The Power of
THANKSGIVING

BARBOUR
PUBLISHING

Published by Barbour Publishing, Inc., P.O. Box 719, Uhrichsville, Ohio 44683, www.barbourbooks.com

Our mission is to publish and distribute inspirational products offering exceptional value and biblical encouragement to the masses.

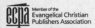 Member of the
Evangelical Christian
Publishers Association

Printed in the United States of America.

INTRODUCTION

Every year we celebrate in abundance—turkey and all the trimmings, decadent slices of pumpkin pie, time spent with family and friends, fellowship, football, and thanks to the One who provides it all.

From the breath in our lungs to the beauty of the sunset, we have much to be thankful for. Honoring God with thanksgiving is something that takes more time and effort than one prayer at one meal, one day a year. Thanksgiving is a powerful act of sacrificial worship that should be a part of our daily lives. Scripture says that God's will is for us to give thanks in every situation (1 Thessalonians 5:18). The Bible also tells us that offering thanks to God truly honors Him (Psalm 50:23).

He's worthy of all the thanks we can offer.

"But giving thanks is a sacrifice that truly honors me.
If you keep to my path, I will reveal to you
the salvation of God."
PSALM 50:23 NLT

Thankful for All

Thou preparest a table before me in the presence of mine enemies: thou anointest my head with oil; my cup runneth over.
PSALM 23:5

Some people never find satisfaction in the things they do have, but spend their entire lives wishing for things they don't have. They are never happy with where their lives are going; they feel empty in their relationships, and therefore they find it impossible to give thanks for the many blessings they have been given.

As Christians, we are to be people of praise. Every prayer we offer unto God should acknowledge the many wonderful things that He has done for us. Not even a blind person can deny the beauty and splendor of this world. God gives good things to His children, and we should be thankful for all that we have.

Lord, I cannot believe how much I have been given. Help open my eyes to the many blessings that have been bestowed upon me. Make me thankful, Lord. Amen.

Satisfaction Guaranteed

Oh, satisfy us early with Your mercy,
That we may rejoice and be glad all our days!
PSALM 90:14 NKJV

You've probably bought items that guaranteed you'd be satisfied. If you weren't, the manufacturer promised, you could get your money back. But how many people bought an item, weren't satisfied, and found the company didn't live up to that promise? We've often found, to our discouragement, that people aren't what they seem and disappear as soon as they've cashed the check or processed the credit card information.

But God isn't like that. He's always what He says He is, and He's gone to great lengths to tell us about Himself. He even sent His Son to clearly show us what He's like. Jesus died for us to give a clear picture of how much He wanted to share our love.

Earthly guarantees often don't give us satisfaction, but when we read His Word and get to know His Son, we quickly comprehend the difference between people's promises and God's. Even when the rest of the world disappoints us, we can cling to Jesus and be glad to the very end.

Have you experienced God's mercy and accepted His love? Then your satisfaction is guaranteed. He promises you'll never be left or forsaken (Hebrews 13:5). Joy in Him will be your portion for the rest of your life.

Impossible Tasks

So the wall was completed on the twenty-fifth of Elul, in fifty-two days. When all our enemies heard about this, all the surrounding nations were afraid and lost their self-confidence, because they realized that this work had been done with the help of our God.

NEHEMIAH 6:15–16 NIV

Under Nehemiah's leadership, the people of Judah had rebuilt Jerusalem's wall in fifty-two days. Facing opposition had only spurred them on. Though half the workers had to stand by fully armed to fend off attack, they'd accomplished their mission. In record time, the wall was standing.

The nations around Judah didn't like it one bit. But it wasn't because of something powerful about the people of Judah—no, they feared this nation because it was clear God had helped them.

Do you face an impossible task today? Perhaps you need to get some work done before the end of the day, and you don't see how you'll do it. Start by asking for God's help, then work as hard as you can, giving your best. But when it's all done, don't expect that you have no more to do. Give God the praise in a tactful way. Perhaps you only need to say, "That was an answer to prayer," but somehow let the message that God was with you be known.

Thank You, Lord, for helping me with impossible tasks.
To You, nothing is impossible.

Reasons to Give Thanks

FOOD ON OUR TABLE
And having food and raiment
let us be therewith content.
1 TIMOTHY 6:8

GOD-GIVEN TALENTS
But now hath God set the members every one
of them in the body, as it hath pleased him.
1 CORINTHIANS 12:18

A PLACE TO WORSHIP GOD
I was glad when they said unto me,
Let us go into the house of the LORD.
PSALM 122:1

God's Handiwork

And the heavens shall praise thy wonders, O LORD:
thy faithfulness also in the congregation of the saints.
PSALM 89:5

The rainstorm had been terrific. Torrents of rain had fallen, drenching everything. Now the clouds began to part. Shafts of bright sunlight stretched to the earth, causing all foliage to sparkle with droplets of water. On the horizon, a rainbow stretched from earth to earth. The clouds climbed high into the sky, turning rosy pink with the sunlight.

God's creation gives testimony to His truth all the time. All His wonders unfold through the course of one day. From the sunrise through nighttime starshine, God's glories unfold. Take time to view God's handiwork. Search the daytime skies and see the majesty of the Almighty. His hand is ever upon His creation.

All praise and honor belongs to You, Lord, for the
magnificent works of your hands. You have made such
beauty, and You have loved us enough to share it.
Thank You, Father. Amen.

He Is Worthy

Offer unto God thanksgiving;
and pay thy vows unto the most High.
PSALM 50:14

Early Christians suffered terrible persecution, even death, for refusing to bow down to idols. Images of Ceasar were prominent throughout the Roman Empire, and all were expected to pay tribute to these graven images. The Christians refused, and so they were thrown into jail, and sometimes they were thrown to wild beasts. God was so important to these early Christians that they could not offer tribute to anyone less worthy.

Only God is worthy to be praised. In all we do and all we are, our lives should pay tribute to God. Nothing else is good enough. Offer to God thanksgiving and praise, for He alone is deserving.

Thank you for the gifts You give, Almighty God. From the
rising of the sun to its setting in the night, I will praise
You for all that You have done. Glory is Yours, Father.
Amen.

Real Thankfulness

Behold, he smote the rock, that the waters gushed out,
and the streams overflowed; can he give bread also?
Can he provide flesh for his people?
PSALM 78:20

Brittany wanted a car, and she got a car. She wanted to go to an expensive college. She wanted her own apartment, and Daddy came through with the money. She wanted nice clothes, a stereo, a cell phone, a microwave, a television. There was no end to Brittany's wants. Nothing satisfied her. No matter how much she was given, she wanted more.

We need to be careful that we don't approach God that way. God wants us to truly appreciate what we have before we start asking for more. He gives good things to His children, and He is willing to give abundantly, but He desires us to learn the real meaning of thankfulness.

Dear God, make me appreciative of all the wonderful
gifts You give. When I take things for granted, show
me the error of my ways. Fill my mind and heart with
gratitude for the many blessings I have. Amen.

Blessed

Honour and majesty are before him:
strength and beauty are in his sanctuary.
PSALM 96:6

Take time to be quiet and think about the good things God has done for you. Look at both the good times and the bad times in proper perspective. We are loved by a God of all creation, the Master of all eternity. He has made us important by His love for us. Think of how wonderful this love is. We have no way to comprehend this kind of love and attention. It is well that we take time to contemplate all these things. All honor and glory belong to the Lord, who loves us so much. By entering into His presence, we come to know just how very blessed we are.

Who am I, Lord, that You take notice of me? I cannot believe that You love me the way You do. Though I don't understand, I do accept Your gracious love, and I am thankful from the depths of my soul. Amen.

Prayers of Thanks

Your Word is my daily nourishment, Lord. Thank You for the Bread of Life that You provide every single day. Those words feed and nurture my soul just as eating bread fills me and provides the nutrition I need to live. Without Your words I will fade and die spiritually; with them I am vibrant, energized, and alive! Be my portion, Lord, as I seek You. And not just Your hands and what You give, but also Your face, Lord. I desire to know who You really are.

Jesus answered, "It is written: 'Man does not live on bread alone, but on every word that comes from the mouth of God.'"
MATTHEW 4:4 NIV

Lord, I thank You for my salvation. I thank You for Your indescribable gift of eternal life and the power to do Your will today. I can hardly fathom how you suffered, yet you did it all for me—for every person on this planet. Mocked and beaten, You bled for my sins. You had victory over death so I could live. You made a way for me, and I am eternally grateful. Thank You, Lord.

Thanks be to God for his indescribable gift!
2 CORINTHIANS 9:15 NIV

Make a Difference

Blessed is he that considereth the poor:
the LORD will deliver him in time of trouble.
PSALM 41:1

*C*urse the beggars! It was impossible to go anywhere without seeing someone with his hand out. Ted refused to look into their faces. He despised people who were always looking for a handout. He worked hard for what he got; why couldn't they? It made him so mad. He rounded the corner and abruptly stopped in front of a young boy who was obviously very ill. The boy looked up into Ted's face and sobbed one word: "Please?"

All the excuses, all the anger, all the contempt melted away. Ted's eyes were opened for the first time. These people really needed help, and he had the power to make a difference. Perhaps he couldn't solve the whole problem, or even a big part, but he could help the boy and his mother. With new resolve, Ted swore to open his eyes to the less fortunate and give as much as he could.

Father, am I doing all I can? In my times of need,
I cry out for someone to help me. Make me
sensitive to others as they cry out. Amen.

Bountiful Harvest

The pastures are clothed with flocks; the valleys also are covered over with corn; they shout for joy, they also sing.
PSALM 65:13

Each year the rice paddies were laid out and the tender plants were planted. Each year the people of the village waited with anxious hope, looking to see whether the storms would come and wash the fields away. Many times, the people would watch as their hard labor was destroyed, but other times they rejoiced to see their crops full and bountiful. After each harvest, the village offered a portion of its harvest to God, thanking Him for His mercy and grace.

What do we offer to God when we are blessed with good things? Do we even remember to say thank you? The Lord has given us so much, and we should always and everywhere give Him thanks and praise.

In bad times, please be my strength; in good times, celebrate with me, Lord. Thanks for being with me, doing so much for me, and giving so much to me. Amen.

Daily Purpose

This is the day which the LORD hath made; we will rejoice and be glad in it.
PSALM 118:24

Rainy days are loved by farmers. Snowy days are loved by children who can stay home from school. Storms are loved by mystery fanatics. Gray days are loved by romantics. Sunny days are loved by picnickers. Warm days are loved by beachgoers. Cool days are loved by those who stroll. All days have their purposes under heaven. Enjoy the day that the Lord has made. He has many more to share.

Let me appreciate the gift of this day, Lord.
Help me to use my time wisely, teach me to rejoice,
and fill me with joy that never ends. Amen.

Beyond Our Asking

More than hearts can imagine or minds comprehend,
God's bountiful gifts are ours without end.
We ask for a cupful when the vast sea is ours
We pick a small rosebud from a garden of flowers,
We reach for a sunbeam but the sun still abides,
We draw one short breath but there's air on all sides
Whatever we ask for falls short of God's giving,
For His greatness exceeds every facet of living
And always God's ready and eager and willing
To pour out His mercy, completely fulfilling
All of man's needs for peace, joy, and rest,
For God gives His children whatever is best.
Just give Him a chance to open His treasures,
And He'll fill your life with unfathomable pleasures—
Pleasures that never grow worn out and faded
And leave us depleted, disillusioned and jaded
For God has a storehouse just filled to the brim
With all that man needs, if we'll only ask Him.

HELEN STEINER RICE

Daily Bread

Blessed be the Lord, who daily loadeth us with benefits,
even the God of our salvation.
PSALM 68:19

When we ask God for our daily bread, what do we mean? Is it merely food to nourish our bodies? Is it all the basic necessities of life? Does it include the bread Jesus spoke of: the Word of God? It is all these things and more. Our heavenly Father wants us to have everything we need to affirm His image within us. God never calls His children to tasks they are not ready for, and He will not abandon us without the resources we need to succeed. Our God provides us with everything we need to be the best people we can be. Call upon the Lord to load you daily with benefits. He will do even more than you expect.

Lord, I do not even know what I need to be better
than I am today, but in Your wisdom, You see my every
need. Give me what You will, in order that I might
honor and glorify You. Amen.

Beautiful Truth

How sweet are thy words unto my taste! yea, sweeter than honey to my mouth!
PSALM 119:103

The singer spun a tale of joy and triumph. The audience sat enthralled by the young woman's voice. She painted a picture lovelier than words. The senses came alive as she performed her art. The sights, sounds, colors, smells, and tastes burst forth through her song. She sang from her heart, and her story was shared by many. Emotions connected, and the entire crowd—singer and audience—moved together in a spiritual harmony. The experience was electrifying.

When we are in the presence of truth and beauty, it is undeniable. There is a chord struck within us all. That chord is the image of God in each of us. We connect with the universal rhythm that God set in time long, long ago. The result is joy—a sensation and a feeling that defies explanation—but assures us of the reality of God. Open yourself to His truth.

There are times when I feel Your presence so strongly, Lord. I know that You have orchestrated a masterpiece of which I am a small but important part. Thank You for including me. Amen.

Immediate Blessings

However, as it is written, "No eye has seen, no ear has heard, no mind has conceived what God has prepared for those who love him."
1 CORINTHIANS 2:9 NIV

God has future blessings in mind for you, but did you realize that this verse is also talking about things you can experience today? Read the context of this passage, and you'll notice that Paul isn't talking about the sweet by-and-by—he's describing his current ministry and the work of the Spirit in the lives of Christians.

If you've been waiting for heaven to enjoy all the joys and delights of faith, look around. Note the blessings you've received today, all the things God has done and is doing in your life, and appreciate them. But don't stop there; you can also start taking advantage of the spiritual mission God has given you. Because God never gives us blessings simply to enjoy—every good thing is meant to be shared.

You don't have to look to another Christian to discover what God has for you. No one in this world can tell you what He has in mind. Verse 10 says God reveals these unseen gifts by His Spirit.

Go to the real source—God. If you ask, He'll show you the gifts He's given and how He wants you to influence others with them.

He has wonderful things in mind for you, so don't wait until eternity—share some of that good news today!

Always Blessed

In the day of prosperity be joyful, but in the day of adversity consider: Surely God has appointed the one as well as the other, so that man can find out nothing that will come after him.
ECCLESIASTES 7:14 NKJV

Sometimes our souls don't feel particularly satisfied. It's hard to feel very peaceful when we lose a job, wonder how we'll pay the rent, and imagine all kind of dire results. Prosperous days seem to lie behind us, and we can't look into the future and tell how long we'll be in this situation.

God doesn't allow us to look into the future. That's a good thing, because if we knew the future, we wouldn't need to trust God. One of His best methods of developing our spiritual lives would no longer exist, and we'd enter heaven as weak, spineless beings—not the strong ones He wants us to become.

But whether our present is joyful or sad, God still remains faithful. He provides for our needs even if we don't get the lavish things we'd prefer. And He always provides generous spiritual blessings for those who trust in Him. Like Paul, who experienced prosperity and want, we can do all things, when we abound in Him (Philippians 4:12–13).

No matter what your circumstances, you can always cling to Jesus—and be blessed.

Reasons to Give Thanks

Time spent conversing with God
I love them that love me: and those
that seek me early shall find me.
Proverbs 8:17

Letters from a loved one
Heaviness in the heart of man maketh it stoop:
but a good word maketh it glad.
Proverbs 12:25

Inspiring, caring teachers
Give instruction to a wise man, and he will
be yet wiser: teach a just man, and he
will increase in learning.
Proverbs 9:9

Accepted by God

"I was sought by those who did not ask for Me;
I was found by those who did not seek Me. I said,
'Here I am, here I am,' To a nation that was
not called by My name."
ISAIAH 65:1 NKJV

None of us was really searching for God when He found us. Though we may have begun to feel empty inside, we didn't know where to go. Then God brought along someone who told us that He loved us and wanted to share our lives with us. We heard the good news that He wanted to heal and forgive us.

We don't come to God with any status. Everyone comes as poor, empty sinners. Out of that, God builds new lives. Do we show that truth in our living? Can we accept others, no matter how rich or poor they are, no matter what background they come from? Or are we haughtier than God, requiring financial "perfection" or a certain "acceptable" background of our friends, fellow church members, and acquaintances?

God sought us—unloved, unappealing, seemingly valueless sinners—and gave us all His love. He saw something in us when no one else could. Can't we do the same for all those who touch our lives?

Thank You, Lord, for accepting me just as I am.
Let me live humbly in Your spirit, with love for all.

God's Help

"First here, then there—you flit from one ally to another asking for help. But your new friends in Egypt will let you down, just as Assyria did before."
JEREMIAH 2:36 NLT

When trouble comes, to whom do you go? Jeremiah saw God's people running all over the ancient Near East, looking for help from various powerful nations. As an unstable political situation threatened Judah, it searched for security—in all the wrong places. As Jeremiah prophesied, the nation was eventually led into exile, because instead of looking to God, it looked to other people (v. 37).

Getting some support from others is a good thing. We all need help at home, on the job, and in the community. And offering help to others is the right thing to do. But there are things no human can help us with—solutions no person can come up with. Ultimately, if we trust our lives to anyone but God, we're looking for safety in the wrong place.

No matter what challenges you face today, have you asked God for help? Whether it's tutoring one of the kids in math or painting the house, have you placed your day in His hands?

If so, you need never despair: He will help you today.

Thank You, Lord, for always being willing to come to my aid. Help me accomplish all I really need to do today.

Strength

A gracious woman retaineth honour:
and strong men retain riches.
PROVERBS 11:16

Judas Iscariot possessed qualities that Jesus considered worthy, or he never would have been selected as a disciple. Judas followed faithfully for the better part of three years, as he shared in the ministry of Christ. At a time when he should have been strongest, he proved weak. He gave in to the temptation of the sparkle of silver, and he betrayed his friend and Lord. He had lived so very close to the true treasure—the love of Jesus Christ, and he threw it all away due to his weakness.

Everyone sins. That is sad, but true. Often we are weak when we want to be strong. It is vital that we hold on to the love of God in those times when we are most sorely tempted. God offers us His strength when our own strength is not enough. When we call on God to help us in our weakness, then we have found true wisdom and strength. If we will deal honestly with God, He will shower us with treasure that cannot be taken from us, and honor that testifies to the glory of Christ.

O Lord, I pray that I might make You proud of me.
I will try to please You by my actions and praise You
with my words. Be with me, Father. Amen.

Prayers of Thanks

Lord, what a blessing that You have given us such an array of emotions with which to express ourselves. Help me to be more like You—slow to anger and abounding in love. Help me to be forgiving. I pray for more discernment, so that in whatever comes my way I will have the grace to think, speak, and act with a good and godly attitude.

> *"The LORD is slow to anger, abounding in love and forgiving sin and rebellion."*
> NUMBERS 14:18 NIV

Lord, I thank You for my home. Show my heart opportunities to open this home to others. I want to share what You've provided for me. As I practice hospitality, may Your love shine through my life. However my home compares to others', I thank You for what I have. I am grateful that Your Spirit is present here. Give me a generous, open heart, and use my home for Your good purposes.

> *Share with God's people who are in need.*
> *Practice hospitality.*
> ROMANS 12:13 NIV

Ours for a While

The earth is the LORD's and the fulness therof;
the world, and they that dwell therein.
PSALM 24:1

Two families disputed for years about who held claim upon a stretch of fertile land. Harsh words and insults were exchanged regularly, and on occasion, tempers flared to the point of physical violence. Neither family would budge in their conviction that they were the rightful owners. No compromise could be reached, and so the seeds of bitterness took root between the two clans.

Long after the two families are but faint memories, the land will still be there. How foolish it is to devote so much of our lives to the acquisition of things, when it all truly belongs to the Lord. We are but caretakers of what the Lord has made, and it has been given to us for everyone's pleasure. Wise use of our resources and preservation of all creation is the responsibility of all humankind. We have been given many precious gifts, but they are ours for only a while. In time, all things return to the Lord.

Lord, make me a wise steward of Your creation.
Let my actions hurt not one living thing.
Help me to build up, rather than destroy.
Inspire me to share, to give, and to love. Amen.

A Faithful Blessing

And he blessed Abram, saying, "Blessed be Abram by
God Most High, Creator of heaven and earth."
GENESIS 14:19 NIV

Read through the story of Abraham and his
family, and you'll find repeatedly the words *bless,*
blessed, or *blessing.* God made it abundantly clear He
wanted to do wonderful things for these people.

Yet sometimes being blessed by God still has its
difficult moments. Abraham and Sarah received a
promise—a child would be theirs, despite the fact
that both were elderly. But time went on, and the
promise wasn't fulfilled. Like most of us, this couple
didn't want to wait. So they decided to take control
of the situation, and Sarah gave her maid, Hagar,
to Abraham. However, the child the maid bore was
not the babe of promise, but a terrible problem for
the little family and the nation it became. It's to
Ishmael, Hagar's son, that the Arab nations trace
their heritage.

God's blessing doesn't mean we can't make mistakes and pay a price for them. Like Abraham, we
can get ourselves in awful trouble. But we can be sure
God will be faithful with His blessing. "The LORD
had blessed [Abraham] in every way," records the
scripture toward the end of Abraham's life (Genesis
24:1). Despite the mistakes, God still loved him and
gave him great blessings.

God has blessed us with a relationship with
Him. He is faithful to us, too. Let us walk faithfully
in His way through all our days.

All Good

Everything God created is good, and nothing is to be rejected if it is received with thanksgiving.
1 TIMOTHY 4:4 NIV

*H*as God given you good things? In our culture, that often implies a huge house, a fancy car, and steak for dinner. But haven't you had a house you loved, even though it wasn't in the finest part of town, an older car you didn't want to get rid of, or a macaroni-and-cheese dinner that fed your stomach and your taste buds as well as any steak? Good things don't have to cost a lot of money.

Your best relationships are priceless. Would you trade a much-loved parent for money or a spouse for gold? These, too, are gifts from the heavenly Father, who knows how to give the best—no matter the cost.

And what of the other things God creates that have no price? A sunset filled with vibrant colors, a drink of water that quenches thirst as no man-made beverage can. God has given generously, in many more ways than we often consider.

But no matter what God gives us, we are to receive it with thanks. He made it just for us, and we're enjoying the benefit, so why not share that joy with Jesus? He's the best gift God had to offer—and the only gift we truly need.

Nice Deal

The LORD also will be a refuge for the oppressed,
a refuge in times of trouble.
PSALM 9:9

Ellen lived in a tiny shack on the edge of a small backwater town. She had no modern conveniences, no car, no electricity, no fancy clothing. She just lived a simple life, sharing what little she did have with anyone who needed it. Often people tried to help Ellen, but she just smiled and said she didn't need anything. When asked why she lived as she did, Ellen said, "God has made sure that I've had enough to get by on. I don't need any more than that. He and I have a nice deal. When He needs me, He lets me know and shows me what I can do; and when I need Him, all I have to do is call. I've faced hard times, but the Lord has always given me strength and given me a place to run to."

The Lord is our refuge and our strength. It takes a great deal of wisdom to realize that. Our lives are much more than possessions and positions. We need not ask what more God can do for us, but what we might do for God.

Father, I sometimes need to escape: from the world,
from myself, from the things that tie me down.
Be my liberation and my sanctuary. Strengthen
me for Your service. Amen.

Reasons to Give Thanks

TIME SPENT WITH FAMILY
*Blessed is everyone that feareth the LORD; that
walketh in his ways. . .Thy wife shall be as a fruitful
vine by the sides of thine house: thy children like
olive plants round about thy table.*
PSALM 128:1, 3

A GODLY MENTOR
*Where no counsel is, the people fall: but in
the multitude of counsellors there is safety.*
PROVERBS 11:14

PRODUCTIVE GARDENS
*Build ye houses, and dwell in them;
and plant gardens, and eat the fruit of them.*
JEREMIAH 29:5

Funny Creatures

Whatsoever the LORD pleased, that did he in heaven, and in earth, in the seas, and all deep places.
PSALM 135:6

Imagine the fun the Lord had creating all the animals of this world. With the power to do whatever He pleased, He concocted a menagerie of some wonderful creatures. Consider the giraffe, or the baboon, or the frog. What a host of funny-looking creatures. Think of the splendor of the eagle, the grace of the gazelle, the power of the tiger. God put so much into making His creation a good one. The same is true of His children. God went to great lengths to make sure His children were good. He even imparted to each and every one of them His own image. He offered them free will and all the blessings they could ever hope for. He did these things because they pleased Him. Our God is a God of love, and nothing pleases Him more than to be able to share that love. Indeed, we may be God's funniest creatures, but that only makes Him love us all the more.

Father, You must have a wonderful sense of humor to put up with children like me. Forgive me for being less than You created me to be. Help me to grow and mature and develop into Your image. Amen.

Best Love

Because your love is better than life,
my lips will glorify you.
PSALM 63:3 NIV

Nothing in this world is better than knowing God. Perhaps, with all the delights of this world, that sounds a little strong. You may be in no rush to enter heaven and lose the things you've worked hard for and the earthly blessings God's given you. But if you can remember back to the days before you knew God, think of the difference He has made. Would you go back to life before Jesus?

Once Jesus enters a heart, losing life becomes but a painful moment that opens the door to eternity. Eternal delights for the Christian cannot compare to anything here on earth—even the best of the blessings God's already given us. Our hearts are no longer earthbound, and we long to be with him. When He calls, we cannot imagine staying in this world without His blessing.

Though we may not rush to leave the fellowship of friends and family, the beauty of the world, and so much more that God has given, like the psalmist, we appreciate that anything that lacks Jesus is less than the best. Life here, without God's love, would be meaningless.

David had his priorities straight when he wrote this. Even being king of Israel, with all its benefits, wasn't better than loving God. So during his life, he praised his Maker. And in eternity, he's praising still.

Basic Needs

O God, thou art my God; early will I seek thee: my soul thirsteth for thee, my flesh longeth for thee in a dry and thirsty land, where no water is.
PSALM 63:1

The rock face extended straight up. Terry was halfway up, and his arms ached. From the ground it hadn't looked nearly so high. The sun was scorching, and all Terry could think of was a cool drink of water. He would give anything to be able to stop and drink, but there was no safe place to do it. The more he thought of water, the worse his thirst got. He comforted himself by thinking the next drink he took would be the best he'd ever had.

We often don't appreciate the simple things in life until we are unable to enjoy them. Clean air, water to drink, food on the table; these things come easily to most of us, and so we are not as thankful as we might be if we didn't have them. Many in our world have to do without. Remember that even the most basic of our needs is met by the loving grace of God. Thank Him for everything He has given you.

For the air that I breathe, the warmth of the springtime sun, the food that nourishes me, and for so much more, I lift my voice in thanks and praise to You, Lord. Amen.

Prayers of Thanks

Lord, I thank You for my good health. It is a blessing. I pray for Your power to sustain me as I take care of myself—by eating healthy food, drinking enough water, and making movement and exercise a part of my daily life. Give me the self-control and motivation I need to make wise choices to support the health of my mind, my spirit, and my body. Please keep me from injury and illness, and keep me safe, I pray.

Say to him: "Long life to you! Good health to you and your household! And good health to all that is yours!"
1 Samuel 25:6 niv

Lord, I thank You for giving me hope. I don't know where I would be without You. I don't know what the future holds, but You give me the ability to be joyful even while I wait—even when I don't understand. Please help me to have a positive attitude and live with a mind-set of patience and courage as You work Your will in my life. Help me to remain faithful in prayer, Lord, and fully committed to You.

Be joyful in hope, patient in affliction, faithful in prayer.
Romans 12:12 niv

Joy and Love

O come, let us sing unto the LORD:
let us make a joyful noise to the rock of our salvation.
PSALM 95:1

The children lined up on the steps to the altar. Their freshly scrubbed faces shone in the morning light. Nervously, they swayed, twitched, and squirmed. The music began, and each child in turn joined in at a point of his or her own choosing. Some sang out boldly, others mouthed the words, while a few ignored the songs altogether and just waved and smiled at Mommy and Daddy. To call the presentation "music" was stretching the point, but to call it a joyful noise was right on target. The spirit of the children was joy and love, and the hearts of all present were captured quickly. The sound rose to the rafters and beyond. The Lord heard that special choir, smiled, and said, "It is good!"

Let the words of my mouth produce a joyful noise,
acceptable to the Lord and glorifying to
Him in all ways. Amen.

Beautiful Conclusion

*Now to him who is able to do immeasurably more
than all we ask or imagine, according to his power
that is at work within us, to him be glory in the
church and in Christ Jesus throughout all generations,
for ever and ever! Amen.*
EPHESIANS 3:20–21 NIV

Have you ever had God answer a prayer you hadn't
even gotten around to praying yet? Maybe the
problem was on your mind. You mulled it over, but
somehow it never made it to your prayers, perhaps
because the world got in the way. By the time you
got to formal prayer, it'd slipped off into mental
oblivion.

Then one day you learned that God had been at
work all along and solved the problem you'd shelved.
The situation came to a beautiful conclusion, without
your having prayed at all. How awful you felt that
you'd never even brought it before the Savior!

None of us should ignore prayer, and it's a good
idea to keep a prayer list at hand; but even when we
fail, God doesn't. We may ponder something without
prayer, yet in His grace He answers even that unspoken
need. He does immeasurably more than we think to
ask for. How much He deserves our praise!

*I praise You, Lord, for doing more than I'd even
think of asking for. I give You all the glory.*

Pleasing to Him

Blessed is every one that feareth the LORD;
that walketh in his ways. For thou shalt eat
the labour of thine hands: happy shalt thou be,
and it shall be well with thee.
PSALM 128:1–2

Jack sat down to supper with his family. Even after twenty years, there was something special about a meal that came from their own farm. Jack could imagine thousands of families sitting down to similar meals of produce from his farm. It made him feel like there was purpose to his life. The work was hard, and there were worries about the future, but it was all worth it. The farm was Jack's life.

Many people find no satisfaction in the work they do. Their lives lack purpose and meaning. But Christians have an alternative source of meaning in their lives. If a Christian does a job—no matter how large or small—to God's glory, that person will find satisfaction. If we do our work without grumbling and with a joyful heart, we are witnesses to His power in our lives, and we are pleasing to Him.

Do not let me be so concerned with the prestige
of my job, or the salary it pays, or what other people
think of it. Instead, assist me to always do the best
that I can, to Your glory, Father. Amen.

He Never Gives Up

Nevertheless my lovingkindness will I not utterly take from him, nor suffer my faithfulness to fail.
PSALM 89:33

Amy tried everything she could to get the little boy to learn to tie his shoes. She had sat with him for hours. There was nothing she could do to make him understand. Finally, she lost all patience and walked off angrily. His shoe-tying education would have to come from someone else with a lot more patience and endurance!

We may give up on each other, but it is comforting to know that God never gives up on us. His offer of forgiveness is open to us today and every day to come. Even though we reject the offer or do things that are frustrating and displeasing to Him, He never gives up. He asks us daily to follow Him, until the day we finally do. Thank goodness His patience is without bounds.

Though I push the patience of others to the limits, I am glad to know that I have not pushed Yours, Lord. Continue to forgive me, Lord. I am weak and foolish, and only Your great love keeps me going. Amen.

Reasons to Give Thanks

GOD'S PROMISES
The Lord is not slack concerning his promise, as some men count slackness; but is longsuffering to us-ward.
2 PETER 3:9

THE DIVERSITY OF THE FOUR SEASONS
Thou hast set all the borders of the earth: thou hast made summer and winter.
PSALM 74:17

A VOICE TO SING SONGS
I will be glad and rejoice in thee: I will sing praise to thy name, O thou most high.
PSALM 9:2

God's Triumphs

Not unto us, O LORD, not unto us, but unto thy name give glory, for thy mercy, and for thy truth's sake.
PSALM 115:1

Max had worked at the mission for over forty years. There had been weeks on end when he hadn't even gotten to go home. He lived to serve the poor and homeless in his area. When he finally decided to retire, the entire city pitched in to pay him tribute. Throughout the proceedings, Max seemed uncomfortable, and finally he stood to speak.

"I don't want to seem ungrateful, but all this really isn't necessary; and besides, I don't really deserve it. God is the One who needs to be honored. I have just been fortunate enough that He has used me all these years. I really haven't done anything special; I just did what God wanted me to do."

It is difficult to set aside our own egos in order to serve God freely. When all is said and done, however, all that we are able to do is made possible by God's grace. Our triumphs are God's triumphs. Like Max, we should feel privileged that God has chosen to work with us and through us.

Use me, Lord. With the gifts and talents You bestowed upon me, enable me to spread Your good news to everyone I meet. Amen.

A Perfect Gift

*The LORD is my strength and my shield; my heart
trusts in him, and I am helped. My heart leaps for
joy and I will give thanks to him in song.*
PSALM 28:7 NIV

Have you ever felt as if you should give thanks, but
your heart just wasn't in it? Perhaps at Christmas-
time you received a gift that was somehow less than
perfect.

Giving thanks on such an occasion becomes difficult. The giver may suspect you aren't thrilled with the
gift. But you still try to express the appreciation you
do feel.

God never gives us the wrong gift. He never
wraps up another item of clothing to fill our already
overstuffed drawers. Instead, He recognizes the in-
tangibles we never have enough of and presents them
at the moment of need. When we lack strength or
protection, His is there for us.

A much needed gift received at the perfect
moment is always welcome, even if it comes at no
special holiday. God knows that—and understands
the importance of timing for everything He gives.
His presents are always timely, always perfect, and
are certain to be received with thanks by a heart
that's truly His.

Your heart jumps with joy at His presents, doesn't
it? Then, whether you sing His praises or just pray
them quietly, make sure to thank Him for each gift.

Beyond Our Comprehension

Great is our Lord, and of great power:
his understanding is infinite.
PSALM 147:5

The snow was falling in clumps. The blizzard had begun six hours ago, and the world had ground to a halt, at least, the world in northeast New York State. It was astonishing to watch the snow accumulate: not into mounds, but into mountains. Somewhere, Stuart had learned in his childhood that no two snowflakes were ever the same. Incredible! The Lord never ceased to create. Billions of snowflakes fell to earth, and not one matched any other. How could people doubt that some creative force was behind the universe?

When we stop to admire the many miracles in nature, we are met with the indisputable evidence of a mastermind who brought everything into being. The power of the Lord is beyond our comprehension, and His wisdom and understanding are beyond our knowing. We should be thankful that the Lord has given us so much beauty. We are blessed by the Lord's continuing creativity.

Dear Father, you have shared so many good things
with me. Let me fully appreciate them all. Show me
the wonders of this world, and let me receive them with
the wonder and amazement of a child. Amen.

Prayers of Thanks

Lord, I thank You for the joy of answered prayer! You are amazing. I delight in You and thank You with a full heart. I asked and You answered. I receive what You give with a grateful heart. Lord, You are good. You are faithful. You are my joy and my delight. I praise Your holy name. Thank You for filling my heart with gladness, Lord.

"Until now you have not asked for anything
in my name. Ask and you will receive,
and your joy will be complete."
JOHN 16:24 NIV

Lord, I thank You for the work of Your hands. A wildflower, a mountain scene, the ocean waves on a white sandy beach—the beauty of the earth reveals Your glory. Thank You for the smile of a child, the touch of my beloved's hand, the warmth of our home. I am grateful for the love of friends and meaningful work. You have done great things for us, and we are filled with joy. Thank You for Your many blessings.

The LORD has done great things for us,
and we are filled with joy.
PSALM 126:3 NIV

Why Give Thanks?

Give thanks to the LORD, for he is good;
his love endures forever.
1 CHRONICLES 16:34 NIV

It's not hard to accept that even something God says *once* in scripture is meaningful. But what does it mean when He tells us the same thing over and over? The words of this verse appear dozens of times.

Think God's trying to get something critical through to us?

Though God tells us repeatedly that He is good and His love never ends, it's strange, isn't it, that every time a war starts, we start questioning that first assertion. Is God really good if bad things happen? Has His love changed? If life isn't going our way, we easily ignore the culpability of humans and throw the blame right on God.

Maybe God repeated this scripture so often because He knows how badly we need it. Satan has such an easy time tricking us that we need to keep reality directly in front of us. So over and over, God reminds us of His true nature.

This is a good verse to memorize, because when Satan starts attacking, we can ask ourselves, *Why should we give thanks to the Lord?* And we'll have the answer, *For He is good and His love endures forever.*

Good Thoughts

Oh that men would praise the LORD for his goodness,
and for his wonderful works to the children of men!
PSALM 107:21

Jay was one of the most unpopular men in the office. He never had a good word to say to anyone. He was critical, snide, self-centered, and jealous. People simply got tired of hearing all the negative comments coming from his mouth. Just once they wanted to hear something good come from his lips.

Negative people get on our nerves quickly. They get on God's nerves, too. He calls us to praise Him and lift our voices in positive ways. If only more people would praise the Lord for His goodness, what a wonderful place our world would become. We need to occupy our thoughts with what is good and turn away from what is bad. Praise God throughout the day and see what wonderful feelings you find along the way.

Erase from my vocabulary all negative words and
from my mind all negative thoughts, Lord. Create
in me a fountain of positive feeling and goodwill.
Share your grace through my witness. Amen.

With Every Breath

Let every thing that hath breath praise the LORD.
Praise ye the LORD.
PSALM 150:6

God looked down upon His creation and saw that it was good. In time, God's creation looked back and saw that God was good. Together they formed a unity of love and devotion. Through their covenant, all creation was brought into harmony. The Lord loves His children, and many of His children love Him back. Praise the Lord with all of your being. With each breath you take, remember that the Lord is God. Nothing you do is done apart from Him. Wherever you go, God is there. He will never leave those who love Him. He gives us new years and new challenges, and He helps us to grow and learn. We can enter new phases of life confident that God goes forth with us. Praise the Lord, one and all. The Lord has been very good to His children.

I thank you for the challenges and joys of yesterday and today. Now I look forward to the future, asking Your blessing upon it. Be with me, Lord, and with all my loved ones. Keep me in your care. Shine Your light upon my path, and make me acceptable in Your sight. Amen.

Choose Happiness

A merry heart maketh a cheerful countenance.
PROVERBS 15:13

You never get mad. You always seem to be happy and having a good time. I don't understand it. I wish I could be like you." The two walked along the beach together. "It's really not that hard. You just have to decide that you're going to be happy, then do it. I got tired of being unhappy about everything, so I decided to quit," the other answered.

We can decide to be happy. It takes work, but it is a conscious effort that anyone can make. God is the giver of the greatest joy a person can ever know. When we make Him the Lord of our life, He can work within us to fill us with this unspeakable joy. The Lord dwells in joy, and He is well at home in a heart that is happy. When we are truly filled with joy, the whole world can see it. They will notice that we are not like everyone else, and there is no more powerful testimony to the power of God than a smile which cannot be taken away.

Fill my heart with Your joy, O Lord. Change the light of my countenance to happiness so that everyone will know the effect You have had on my life. I praise You for Your gracious gift. Amen.

A Thankful Heart

Take nothing for granted, for whenever you do,
The joy of enjoying is lessened for you.
For we rob our own lives much more than we know
When we fail to respond or in any way show
Our thanks for the blessings that daily are ours—
The warmth of the sun, the fragrance of flowers,
The beauty of twilight, the freshness of dawn,
The coolness of dew on a green velvet lawn,
The kind little deeds so thoughtfully done,
The favors of friends and the love that someone
Unselfishly gives us in a myriad of ways,
Expecting no payment and no words of praise.
Oh, great is our loss when we no longer find
A thankful response to things of this kind.
For the joy of enjoying and the fullness of living
Are found in the heart that is filled
with thanksgiving.

HELEN STEINER RICE

Closer Than a Brother

*A friend loveth at all times, and a
brother is born for adversity.*
PROVERBS 17:17

He couldn't believe it. He had worked for the same
company for almost thirty years, and suddenly
they pulled the rug out from under him. He had been
a good employee, and he had never made trouble.
Now he felt ashamed for no good reason. He didn't
know what he would do.

When he saw his brother at his door later that
day, tears came to his eyes. Whenever anything had
ever gone wrong, his older brother had been there to
make him feel better. No matter what happened, he
knew he could always count on his brother. He had
yet to face any bad situation without his brother to
support him, and as long as he could lean on him, he
knew everything would be fine.

As children of God, we can be thankful that we
have Christ to call a brother. He will be with us in every
situation. He will be our support and our counselor.
He will listen without judging and will never leave
us. He is as true as any brother could be, and we can
count on Him to be there for us no matter what.

*Thank You for being there when I need You.
You are my strength and my shield.
I am so grateful for Your love. Amen.*

Totally Blessed

*Dear friend, I pray that you may enjoy good
health and that all may go well with you,
even as your soul is getting along well.*
3 JOHN 2 NIV

When the apostle John wrote his friend Gaius,
he not only wished spiritual blessings on him,
but he prayed for his health and that his life would
go well, too.

It's easy for us to become so spiritually minded
that we forget people's other needs. Because we
know faith is the most important thing, we pray for
a friend's spiritual condition, but do we also pray that
physical needs would be met? Do we ask God to help
the new widow financially and emotionally, as well
as spiritually? Or do we see that as the responsibility
of others? Even if we know she doesn't know Jesus,
do we reach out in concrete love that can touch her
life in other ways?

God's blessings begin with the spiritual, but they
don't end there. We've often had reason to praise Him
because He has provided for our physical needs, time
and time again.

Just as God recognizes the needs of this world,
we should, too. We can't separate the body from the
soul, and often it's the body's needs that make people
aware of a spiritual emptiness. God deals with every
phase of our lives, and as we offer Jesus to others, we
can do that, too.

Then they can learn what it means to be totally
blessed.

The Real Treasure

Keep thy heart with all diligence;
for out of it are the issues of life.
PROVERBS 4:23

Jesus said, "Where your treasure is, there will your heart be also" (Matthew 6:21). Moral poverty occurs when we place things above relationships. Christ sent His disciples out into the world without possessions, but no one in history has known more wealth than those chosen men who walked with Jesus. It is when we walk with Jesus that we discover what true riches are.

It is easy to get distracted by so many things. The "good life" requires money, good looks, nice clothes, the right car, the right house, and the right mate. At least that's what we're led to believe. But it is only when we can free ourselves from the pursuit of such things that we can begin to enjoy life the way God intended it. Money cannot buy happiness, nor can it bring us life. Christ brings us life, and He brings it most abundantly. He is the real treasure, and as long as our hearts remain with Him, our lives will truly be rich.

Dear Father, forgive me when I lose sight of what
is really important in life. Help me to keep my eyes
focused on Your truth. Enable me to show others that
You are the real treasure in life. Amen.

Reasons to Give Thanks

SUNSHINE AFTER STORMS

*The day is thine, the night also is thine: thou hast
prepared the light and the sun.*
PSALM 74:16

THE ABILITY TO LEARN

*A wise man will hear, and will increase learning; and a
man of understanding shall attain unto wise counsels.*
PROVERBS 1:5

KIND WORDS

*A man hath joy by the answer of his mouth: and a word
spoken in due season, how good is it!*
PROVERBS 15:23

Wise Counsel

I lead in the way of righteousness. . .that I may
cause those that love me to inherit substance.
PROVERBS 8:20–21

A poor woman called her children to her soon before her death. She sat them down and told them, "I never had money or nice things, and I'm sorry that I don't have good things to leave you, but I always tried to do what was right by you. If I brought you up right, so that you do what you know is right to do, then I have left you more than any amount of money."

The woman was right. The things money buys are temporal; they wear out, break down, and then they're gone. A good sense of values is worth more than all the money in the world. The greatest gift we can hope to give another human being is that of wise counsel. We often hope that we can leave a legacy—a testament to our life—after we die. We can make our lives an example of the truth of Christ, letting others see just how much Christ can change lives for the better. That is the real treasure, and God gives it freely to all who will take it.

I try to turn my eyes from material gain to true
gain: the gain of eternal life. Help me to follow Your
instructions, that I might have Your righteousness.
Grant me a small portion of Your holy inheritance.
Amen.

True Joy

There is that scattereth, and yet increaseth;
and there is that withholdeth more than is meet,
but it tendeth to poverty.
PROVERBS 11:24

During the Great Depression, two families shared a house in Pennsylvania. One family occupied the upper floor, and the other family lived in the lower. The family that lived downstairs was always inviting people in to share what they had. No matter how much they gave, they always seemed to have enough. The family on the upper floor, however, scoffed at the way the downstairs family lived. They stored all extras in a locker in the pantry and gave nothing away. It was not until they found that rats had gotten into their pantry that they were sorrowful for what they had done.

Selfishness leads to despair. True joy comes to us, not from what we own, but from what we are able to give to others. When we give what we have, God will bless us with more, and the blessings will be doubled because of the joy that giving brings.

Take what I have, Lord, and use it for Your glory.
I have nothing except what You have given me.
Help me to share from my abundance, and to give
all that I can to those who are in need. Amen.

Good Things

I know that nothing is better for them than to rejoice,
and to do good in their lives, and also that every man
should eat and drink and enjoy the good of all his
labor—it is the gift of God.
ECCLESIASTES 3:12–13 NKJV

When God gives you a good thing—a new house,
a child, or a special job—do you hesitate to enjoy
it? Do you feel guilty because you have something
another person doesn't have?

Where does the idea that Christians should not
enjoy life come from? Not from the Bible. Scripture
often speaks of the blessings God gives His people—
and some are physical.

That doesn't mean enjoyment is our primary
goal in life. We shouldn't mainly seek out wealth and
fortune. God describes these things as fleeting, and
putting our trust in them will only lead to sorrow.

But that also doesn't mean we shouldn't rejoice
when God gives us worldly goods or that we shouldn't
make wise use of them. When we thank God for His
blessings and use them properly—to help others
and support our families in a responsible Christian
lifestyle—those temporary things become blessings
He can use through us. That's just what God intended.

If you work hard for your money and are rewarded,
you can appreciate God's gift and use it for blessing.
Then you'll have done right and won't be the only one
who rejoices.

Legacies

What profit is there in my blood, when I go down to the pit? Shall the dust praise thee? shall it declare thy truth?
PSALM 30:9

Most people want to be well remembered when they die. We want to leave a legacy of some kind. What will our legacy be? Will it be money or a building or a statue? Will it be something that will last a short while and be gone? Why can't we leave something truly important?

The greatest legacy we can leave is a life well lived. As Christians, we need to be examples of how wonderful Christ can be. We can honestly usher in the kingdom of God on earth if we will devote ourselves to leading kingdom lives. There is profit in the blood of a Christian. Christ's own blood was shed that we might all inherit eternal life. If God was willing to shed His own blood for us, should we be willing to do any less? God's legacy to us is life eternal. What will our legacy to others be?

May each day I live be considered a gift, Father. Guide me so that I can live each gift to the fullest. Let others see You through me, I pray. Amen.

Prayers of Thanks

Lord, I thank You that I can have a calm spirit—because You are the Prince of Peace. Your name, Jesus, has the authority to make fear and worry flee. Your name has power! You are called Wonderful Counselor because You freely give wisdom and guidance. You are the Mighty God, the One who made the entire world and keeps it all going. My Everlasting Father, it's Your love and compassion that sustain me. I worship and honor You.

And he will be called Wonderful Counselor,
Mighty God, Everlasting Father, Prince of Peace.
ISAIAH 9:6 NIV

Lord, I am so grateful that I know You—and I am learning more about Your character every day. You are holy and sovereign and righteous and just. You are loving and faithful and always good. When I know the One I believe and have a strong conviction that He is willing and able to help me, I can have more peace. You *want* to help me! My God will take care of me. Thank You, Lord.

I know whom I have believed, and am convinced
that he is able to guard what I have
entrusted to him for that day.
2 TIMOTHY 1:12 NIV

Breath of Life

By the word of the LORD were the heavens made;
and all the host of them by the breath of his mouth.
PSALM 33:6

With a simple breath—inhale and exhale—the Lord brought magnificence into creation. The stars and planets that revolve through space came forth on the breath of the Lord. The hosts, heavenly and earthly, sprang from His mouth. Our world and every last thing in it came into being by His Word. How can the splendor and mystery of our God ever be denied? Our Lord is above all things, and there is nothing that is beyond His control. His breath is within us: the breath of all life. Rejoice!

Creator, Your imagination has yielded wonders beyond comprehension. We stand in awe before Your mighty power. Thank You for finding a place in all of this for me. Your love shines forth throughout all of Your creation. Praise be unto You! Amen.

Heaven on Earth

There is a river, the streams whereof shall
make glad the city of God, the holy place
of the tabernacles of the most High.
PSALM 46:4

In the woods of Maine, not too far from the eastern
coast, there is a river that flows clear and cool. It
winds through some of the most gorgeous scenery
imaginable and carries with it a beauty that is
unsurpassed. To see such sights convinces a person of
the reality of God. God gives us glimpses of heaven
here on earth, so that we might long for such a place
from the deepest reaches of our hearts. That part
of us that carries the seed of God responds to His
beauty in creation. If we look at the world with our
spiritual eyes rather than our physical eyes, we will
begin to see God's glories in many new ways. The
gifts of God are indeed abundant. Open your eyes
and enjoy them all.

I stand in awe of the wonder of Your creation, God.
Help me to see beauty wherever I look. Don't let
me waste time on ugliness, but turn my
attention to what is good. Amen.

The Real Thing

For a day in thy courts is better than a thousand. I had rather be a doorkeeper in the house of my God, than to dwell in the tents of wickedness.
PSALM 84:10

Mike had seen pictures of most of the places he visited before he went. Even so, he was not prepared for the beauty he found. Pictures failed to show the magnitude somehow. Traveling across the country brought everything into sharp focus. Being in it was a thousand times better than just seeing pictures of it.

Nothing beats the real thing. Once we are touched by the grace of God, nothing else compares. What this world has to offer us is but a snapshot of what we can really have. The real thing is best. Embrace God and all that He is and all that He does. You'll never need anything else.

Lord, nothing can compare with You. In my life
I have experienced wonderful things, but none so
wonderful as Your love. Thank You. Amen.

Reasons to Give Thanks

THE INNOCENCE OF CHILDREN
*But Jesus said, Suffer little children,
and forbid them not, to come unto me:
for of such is the kingdom of heaven.*
MATTHEW 19:14

PEACEFUL SLEEP
*I will both lay me down in peace, and sleep: for thou,
LORD, only makest me dwell in safety.*
PSALM 4:8

TEARS EXPRESSING OUR JOY OR GRIEF
They that sow in tears shall reap in joy.
PSALM 126:5

Don't Forget the Source

When you have eaten and are satisfied, praise the
LORD your God for the good land he has given you.
DEUTERONOMY 8:10 NIV

God cared for His people throughout their journey to the Promised Land. Whatever trials they
faced, they came through with His help, though they
sometimes failed to recognize that truth. Whether
it was manna in the desert or clothes that lasted for
forty years, He never let them lack for anything they
truly needed.

As the Israelites came to the Promised Land,
God knew that all the good things they'd find there
would distract them from Him. When the food
required their own efforts, instead of coming directly
from His hand, they'd be inclined to believe it
resulted only from their planting and harvesting the
crop. They'd forget who provided rain and made the
plants grow. So God reminded them that thanks were
in order when they ate. Everything really came from
the same God who'd brought them out of the wilderness into this rich land.

It's the same with us. When we face lean times
and have to pray for every meal, we appreciate God's
faithfulness. When the paycheck is slim, we clearly
see that God has provided for the rent, the heat, and
our clothes. But when our paychecks grow or our
investments show good returns, it's easy to forget
God is still providing. No matter where the money
or food comes from, the same Lord provides.

A Joyful Noise

*I will be glad and rejoice in You; I will
sing praise to Your name, O Most High.*
PSALM 9:2 NKJV

Did you know that God doesn't care how good your singing voice is—He still loves to hear it lifted in praise? Whether you're another Luciano Pavarotti or can't carry a tune in a bucket, God rejoices in the praises of His people, and that includes you!

So don't worry how you sound when you lift up your voice at home or in the church. It doesn't matter if you can't read music or can sight-read perfectly. Don't waste time critiquing yourself or worrying what others think. Instead, rejoice with the psalmist at the wonder of God's love. Even if your neighbors or family don't appreciate your voice, you're really singing to an audience of one: God. And He appreciates every note that shows how much you love Him.

*Lord, I praise You! I'm so happy to be Your child,
loved by an omnipotent Father who cares
about the praises I have to offer.*

Spiritual Competition?

I always thank God for you because
of his grace given you in Christ Jesus.
1 CORINTHIANS 1:4 NIV

When God gives another, younger Christian a great blessing, are you thankful or jealous? Paul felt thankful that a powerful blessing had fallen on the Corinthians. Though they were still young believers and didn't have it all together, the correction Paul administered in his letter to them was not done from a sense of jealousy. A few years later, the apostle let them know he wasn't interested in making himself famous, but in lifting up Jesus. From one who had worked to develop thriving churches on two continents, his sense of humility is amazing.

God doesn't give any of us blessings to start a game of "Who Can Top This?" Realizing the futility of such desires, Paul committed himself to doing the real job—reaching people for Jesus—instead of trying to make himself look good.

Is there a new Christian in your church who's doing great things for God, even though he doesn't know the scriptures as well as you do? Come alongside him and encourage him. Offer to help him however you can. Make it a priority to pray for him. Then thank God for the blessings He's given you, too, and make the most of your gifts, so that together you can lead people to Jesus.

In His Footsteps

Then they said to her, "Woman, why are you weeping?"
She said to them, "Because they have taken away my
Lord, and I do not know where they have laid Him."
JOHN 20:13 NKJV

Faithful Mary Magdalene didn't quite understand. Still she looked for Jesus' body. To her, the Master's disappearance must have seemed one big hoax, perhaps the work of the religious leaders who wanted to get rid of Him any way they could.

The alternative did seem pretty preposterous. What man who died that kind of painful criminal's death came back to life? Crucifixion was a particularly nasty way to end your life, and for that reason, people who died that way were not considered blessed by God. Jesus seemed to be the last person who would receive life again.

Sometimes the people God saves seem to be in the same situation. The "nice" folks we'd love to see come to Him don't. But that onetime biker or gang member does. God doesn't deal in the probabilities that something will be true or false. He works in His own way. What seems impossible one day is a glorious fact the next.

That's the way it was when Jesus was raised from death into new life. We only follow in His footsteps.

Thank You, Lord, for bringing one as impossible
as I to new life. I glory in Your work in my life.

Prayers of Thanks

Lord, I am thankful for the financial resources with which You have blessed me. I want to be a good steward, a wise manager, of the resources You have entrusted to me. Help me to save and spend with discernment and to give to others in need. Help me to find balance—not be a hoarder or an out-of-control spender. Give me a godly view of money and show me how to use it in ways that will honor You.

Now it is required that those who have been given a trust must prove faithful.
1 CORINTHIANS 4:2 NIV

Lord, I thank You for Your blessings. Whether in plenty or with little, I want to be a cheerful giver. I desire to give from a full heart that serves, not reluctantly or with complaining. I long to see Your money used in ways that will bless others—through my tithing at church or giving to mission organizations or helping the needy. I choose to give at whatever level I can—and ask You to bless it.

Each man should give what he has decided in his heart to give, not reluctantly or under compulsion, for God loves a cheerful giver.
2 CORINTHIANS 9:7 NIV

He Chose You

And the blood shall be to you for a token upon the houses where ye are: and when I see the blood, I will pass over you, and the plague shall not be upon you to destroy you, when I smite the land of Egypt.
EXODUS 12:13

On Passover, the Jews did as God commanded and painted the blood of a lamb on their doorposts and lintel. He had promised them that when the angel of death went through Egypt, killing the firstborn children and animals, any house having such a mark would be passed by.

Like those ancient Jews, we too have been passed over, though not through the blood of a sheep. The blood shed for us was much more precious—that of God's Son. Where the lamb's blood saved only one nation, Jesus' blood has touched people throughout the world, from every nation and tribe imaginable—including ours.

While we deserved death, God has passed by us because of His Son. Are we awed by that truth? Has it changed the way we live, work, and act? If not, have we asked ourselves, "Out of the whole world, why would God choose me?" If that does not humble us, do we know what Jesus' death means?

Lord, I'm amazed that you had such mercy on me. Thank You for Your gift of life.

Stop and Give Thanks

*"Go out of the ark, you and your wife,
and your sons and your sons' wives with you."*
GENESIS 8:16 NKJV

Hearing these words must have ranked as one of the most wonderful moments in Noah's life. A praise party probably followed Noah's announcement that it was time to leave behind their cruise ship and step again on dry land.

The first thing Noah did, once they and the animals had left the ark, was to build an altar and worship God. How many levels of appreciation he must have felt: first, for the safety of him, his family, and the animals; then gratitude that they could finally leave what by then must have been a very smelly, noisy place. How Noah and family must have looked forward to their new life.

When we come to a happy turning point in our lives, do we rush to thank God? Or do we assume that our own abilities have brought us this far and take the credit for ourselves? We've never stepped foot on an ark, but He's surely cared for us, too.

*Thank You, Lord, for every time You've saved me
and kept me from harm. I praise You for being the
compassionate One who guides my life each day.*

Jesus Doesn't Forget

And Samuel said unto Jesse, Are here all thy children?
And he said, There remaineth yet the youngest, and,
behold, he keepeth the sheep. And Samuel said unto
Jesse, Send and fetch him: for we will not sit down till
he come hither.
1 SAMUEL 16:11

None of us likes to be forgotten or thought of as unimportant. Even though we may deny it and like to be thought of as independent, others' opinions count to us. We want people to respect our ideas and even seek them out. When there's an honor to be handed out, we'd like to be considered for it, whether it's a promotion or an award.

But even King David had a time when he was forgotten. Out watching sheep—a lowly job—David was out of the way. When the prophet Samuel asked Jesse to see his sons, the father forgot his youngest son. Who would imagine this boy as a king? No one in the family saw the promise in the youth who became a successful warrior and ruler.

Just because others don't see your promise, don't give up. God sees when others are blinded by their humanity. His wonderful, promise-filled future does not rely on human ideas of your value.

Even if the whole world forgets or ignores you, Jesus doesn't.

Lord, thank You for remembering
me when the world forgets.

Reasons to Give Thanks

TWO HANDS TO PERFORM TASKS
Whatsoever thy hand findeth to do, do it with thy might; for there is no work, nor device, nor knowledge, nor wisdom, in the grave, whither thou goest.
ECCLESIASTES 9:10

LAUGHTER TO EXPRESS OUR JOY
Then was our mouth filled with laughter, and our tongue with singing: then said they among the heathen, The LORD hath done great things for them.
PSALM 126:2

THE ACT OF FORGIVENESS
And be ye kind one to another, tenderhearted, forgiving one another, even as God for Christ's sake hath forgiven you.
EPHESIANS 4:32

His Hand in Everything

*In every thing give thanks: for this is the will
of God in Christ Jesus concerning you.*
1 THESSALONIANS 5:18

Busy days are best organized by God. Over and over, that truth becomes apparent when you offer up your day to God and a light appears at the end of the tunnel for a seemingly impossible problem. By the end of the day, you've accomplished a lot.

But when the day works out because you've prayed briefly (though perhaps frequently), do you take the credit for yourself, thinking, *I'm glad I worked it all out*, or do you recognize why it worked out in the end and thank the One who smoothed the way for you?

Not thanking God is a terrible oversight—and one that may be very easy to do. Remembering to thank God in an impossible situation, as when a friend or loved one is so ill the doctors can't help, isn't hard. We recognize our limitations and quickly thank Him when we hear the good news of healing. But a heart that's open to Him gradually recognizes His hand in everything, even the small things.

So when your day goes better than expected, thank Him. He's always glad to hear words from a grateful heart.

*Lord, thank You for making every day a better one.
Just knowing You eases my entire life.*

Depend on God

Have mercy upon me, O LORD; for I am weak:
O LORD, heal me; for my bones are vexed.
PSALM 6:2

The closer we get to God, the more glaring are our faults. The brighter the light of perfection, the more flaws are revealed. The better we understand the awesome magnificence of God, the more we expose our own imperfections. As the great men and women of the Bible came to realize, the stronger we become in the faith, the more wretched we sometimes feel.

This, however, is no cause for despair. Our Lord wants nothing more than for us to come to depend on Him. We can only truly become dependent as we acknowledge our inadequacies. As the apostle Paul found out, true strength comes from admitting our weakness, and total healing comes by realizing that without God we are sickly and terminally diseased by sin. Cry out for the mercy of God, and He will strengthen you; ask for His healing, and you will be made whole.

Dear Lord, I try to be perfect and find that I am
hopelessly deficient. Nothing I can do will bring me the
perfection you intend for me. Fill me with Your Spirit,
and do for me all that I cannot do for myself. Amen.

We Need Each Other

*He poureth contempt upon princes, and causeth them to
wander in the wilderness, where there is no way.*
PSALM 107:40

I don't need any help. I can do everything just fine
on my own!"

Randy shouldered his pack and headed down
the path. Jerry and Tom shook their heads and
followed. Before long, Randy was out of sight, and
his two friends gave up trying to follow. As evening
set in, they made camp and waited for their friend
to return. While they sat by a warm and inviting
fire, Randy stumbled through the dense forest, lost,
alone, and afraid.

We were created for one another. There is no
sense in trying to deny it. Those who attempt to
stand on their own two feet find that they tire before
long, and they wish they had someone to lean on.
God created us equal, so that we can adequately fill
one another's needs. He hopes we will share our lives
with one another and with Him. People who feel they
are above needing others will be shown the error of
their ways in due time. It is better to admit our need
and wander this wilderness with companions who
make the journey a lot more enjoyable.

*Father, I thank You that I never have to walk alone.
You are by my side, and I have opportunities to
share my life journey with so many others.
Bless my path, O Lord. Amen.*

A Time of Blessing

*And I have given you a land for which ye
did not labour, and cities which ye built not,
and ye dwell in them; of the vineyards and
oliveyards which ye planted not do ye eat.*
JOSHUA 24:13

Sometimes things come easily to us. The work
seems to go smoothly, and the rewards seem
even larger than we expected. *What, am I on a roll?*
we may want to ask ourselves.

No, it's not a roll, it's a time of blessing. Sometimes God just seems to let us have so much, we
wonder why He's doing it. Life seems wonderful,
and we can enjoy it. But we can't forget that all this
blessing has a purpose. God doesn't give a promotion
without expecting we'll use our new position wisely.
He doesn't give raises that He expects us to spend
only on ourselves; we need to remember the work of
His church and give accordingly.

Feeling blessed? Have you asked God what you
can do to share that blessing? Then, have you done
what He commanded?

*Thank You, Lord, for the many blessings
You've given me. Today show me how to
use the ones in my hand now.*

Prayers of Thanks

Lord, I thank You for my wonderful friends! As I think about the treasure chest of my close friends, casual friends, and acquaintances, I am grateful for the blessings and the joys each one brings to my life. Thank You for my close friends—those who listen, care, and encourage me. I acknowledge that You, Lord, are the giver of all good gifts, and I thank You for Your provision in my friendships.

A man of many companions may come to ruin,
but there is a friend who sticks closer than a brother.
PROVERBS 18:24 NIV

Lord, I thank You for my family members and those who are like family to me. I am grateful for their love and understanding. May I be loving in return—not only with those who love me, but even with those who are hard to be around. Your ways are merciful and kind, forgiving and good. Help me to reflect Your love, finding joy in loving others as You love me.

"If you love those who love you, what reward will you
get? Are not even the tax collectors doing that?"
MATTHEW 5:46 NIV

Power from God

"Let him who boasts boast in the Lord."
1 CORINTHIANS 1:31 NIV

Are you on a spiritual high? Is life going well for you at home, at the workplace, and in a ministry? Then you may be in a very dangerous place. You may feel tempted to take credit for all those good things. Perhaps you're starting to feel as if you have some special spiritual knowledge that makes you better than others. Or maybe you've reached out to others, they've responded to Jesus, and you're starting to feel you're an outrageous witness for God.

It's great that God is using you so powerfully, but don't forget that He's the One giving you the power to speak those words and that it's His Spirit that's touching the hearts. We are tools in God's hands, and we need to be ready for Him to pick up and use us, but we're not the One who made the plans and brought them to completion.

Praise God for your successes, but remember that without Him, they are impossible. Boast about what happened, if you want, but boast that Jesus did it, not you.

Lord, I want to lift up Your name so others
know what's happening and who caused it.
I could never do this on my own.

Trust in Him

My soul finds rest in God alone;
my salvation comes from him.
PSALM 62:1 NIV

Whom do you really trust? In this life perhaps you have some good friends and family members who are reliable. Maybe you have a few whom you'd prefer to trust carefully because of their past track records. But David tells us that God was the One he *really* trusted in—the One he could trust even with his soul.

Right now, you may trust that your sister will keep your secret, your friend will return the garden tools he borrowed, or that your parents with come through with the down payment on a new home. If these things fell through, it would only affect you for a short time. You'd manage something else or get over it. Yet David's trust is not for a few days, weeks, or months, but for eternity. He has hung his heart on the truth that God will save him, both in this world and the next.

Who are you trusting with your soul today? Some people wrongly trust in tarot readers, psychics, and others as they look to the future. Others assertively deny that there is any future after this life. But everyone is trusting in something. Many bank on sliding into an eternal nothingness, but even they trust that there is no eternity. Where are you looking for your eternity?

Lord, let me trust in You alone.

Ticket to Eternity

Now when a man works, his wages are not credited to him as a gift, but as an obligation. However, to the man who does not work but trusts God who justifies the wicked, his faith is credited as righteousness.
ROMANS 4:4–5 NIV

You probably don't work for free—you need money to live on, pay the rent with, and save for a rainy day. The scriptures recognize that a valuable worker deserves fair recompense.

Though the Bible recognizes the need to earn a living, it also tells us God's kingdom isn't like that. We can't work our way into heaven, because we can't do anything to make ourselves right with God. The only one who can do that is God's perfect Son, Jesus. When we believe that He died in order to forgive our sins, we agree with God on the subject, and our eternal destination becomes heaven. God gives us that gift for doing nothing more than trusting in Him.

Spend time today in worship; and instead of trying to enter heaven on your own credit, you'll arrive there safely on your trust in Jesus. It's the only way you *can* get in.

Thank You, Lord, that I can only enter into heaven by trusting in You. I could work 24/7 and never build up the righteousness You offer as a gift.

Reasons to Give Thanks

FREEDOM OF WORSHIP
I will worship toward thy holy temple,
and praise thy name.
PSALM 138:2

BEAUTIFUL MUSIC TO ENJOY
Sing unto him a new song;
play skillfully with a loud noise.
PSALM 33:3

THE WARMTH OF A FIRE IN WINTER
I will praise thee, O LORD, with my whole heart;
I will shew forth all thy marvelous works.
PSALM 9:1

Heavenly Party

*I say unto you, that likewise joy shall be in heaven over
one sinner that repenteth, more than over ninety and
nine just persons, which need no repentance.*
LUKE 15:7

Has God ever thrown a party for you? Do you
know how much doing that would thrill Him?

When a soul enters eternity by faith in Jesus,
all heaven rejoices over that new member of God's
kingdom. You might say God throws a party just
for the new believer. All heaven celebrates for each
person who comes to God through His Son. If
you know Jesus, there was a day when God gave a
celebration with your name on it. Invitations went
out to all heaven, and everyone had a great time
rejoicing in what God had done in your life. It was a
great day!

If you've never had such a great day in your life,
it can still happen. All you need to do is admit to
God that you need to turn your life around. Tell Him
you know you've sinned and need His forgiveness
and that you're trusting in Jesus for that forgiveness.

Do you hear a party starting?

*Lord, thank You that all heaven rejoices at the salvation
of one person. Thank You that You were willing to
let all heaven celebrate because I came to faith in You.
Amen.*

Reason for Praise

Let everything that has breath praise the LORD.
PSALM 150:6 NKJV

Why is the Bible always telling us to praise God? Is He really stuck on Himself? Or does He need praise to feel good about Himself? Instead, why doesn't God tell us to praise one another—or even share some of our own wonderful qualities with others? Doesn't He like us very much?

These question are actually pretty silly once you realize the kind of God you're talking about. He does not desire praise because He's a weakling. Instead, He tells us to praise Him because by doing that, our hearts recognize His infinite greatness and powerfulness. Only by praise can we recognize who He is and how small we are in comparison. Praise opens our eyes to God's true character. With it we can voice how much we appreciate the world He created for us, the love He freely gives, and the thousands of other graces He offers us.

As we comprehend God's greatness, we more completely appreciate His mercy and love in sending us Jesus. Through Jesus, the all-powerful One stepped into our world and became one of us, though He already owned the entire universe and didn't have to respond.

He only took that step so that He could also own our hearts.

In God's Image

So God created man in his own image, in the image of God created he him; male and female created he them.
GENESIS 1:27

W e hold these truths to be self-evident that all men are created equal," wrote Thomas Jefferson in the Declaration of Independence. Try to write those words in a government document today, and you'd probably take some flak; but Jefferson had no problem in his day because even those, like himself, who were not committed Christians accepted certain facts about God. Though Jefferson himself did not believe in all the scripture, he surely accepted creation as fact.

What wise men accepted several hundred years ago is now doubted by so many. But that has not changed the truth. You *are* created in God's image. Whether you are male or female, He values you deeply. And from Him you have the promise of a potential that goes far beyond your own meager skills and abilities.

Don't let those who doubt discourage you from believing what many of our founding fathers accepted without question. God did make you. You are valuable to Him and "endowed with inalienable rights." Better than the "life, liberty, and the pursuit of happiness" Jefferson propounded, God offers you life eternal with Him.

Willing Children

When I consider thy heavens, the work of thy fingers,
the moon and the stars, which thou hast ordained; what
is man, that thou art mindful of him?
PSALM 8:3–4

A devout man refused to enter a church because he said that he was not worthy to tread on holy ground. Whenever he saw a cross, he burst into tears and turned his eyes away, lamenting that he would never be good enough to hope for salvation.

One day a traveling minister entered the man's hometown. He saw the devout man sitting on the stones outside the church building, and so he stopped to talk. When he found out the man's thoughts, he told him, "God is not looking for worthy men, but willing children. He doesn't want to be surrounded by people trying to impress Him with how much they can love Him. He merely wants people who will receive the great love He has to give. Come, and receive the gift of the Lord. He set the earth and skies in motion, the birds in the air, the fish in the sea, the creatures on the earth; and He did it all for you, my friend."

Though I do not deserve Your great love, Father God,
I thank You that You give it so freely. Embrace me as
a child, cradle me in Your strong and tender arms, and
help me remember that I am Yours. Amen.

Prayers of Thanks

I praise You, Lord, thanking You for this great nation. You have blessed America! Thank You for peace. Thank You for the freedom to speak and be heard and to vote for our leaders. Help us to uphold godly values as we seek to honor the authority of those who govern our land. Please keep the United States united—as one strong country that seeks Your face and favor.

Give thanks to the LORD, call on his name;
make known among the nations what he has done.
PSALM 105:1 NIV

L ord, I thank You for all the men and women serving in our armed forces. They choose to put their lives on the line so we can have freedom and peace—and for that I am truly grateful. Protect them and keep them safe. Comfort them and give them strength when they are away from loved ones. Bless, too, the families who send soldiers to war or for duty overseas. I pray that You would meet their every need, Lord.

The LORD is my strength and my shield;
my heart trusts in him, and I am helped.
PSALM 28:7 NIV

In Control

Jumping up, they mobbed him and forced him to the edge of the hill on which the town was built. They intended to push him over the cliff, but he passed right through the crowd and went on his way.
LUKE 4:29–30 NLT

The people in Jesus' hometown of Nazareth were so angry at Him, they wanted to kill Him. In fact, they took Him to a cliff to throw Him over. A few more minutes, and if He hadn't been God's Son, He would've been history.

But did you miss the most important part of those verses? Jesus just slips away. An irate mob, and He just walks through it as if it were water. No one stops Him. No one questions Him. In a few minutes, He's on His way. Jesus' whole life—and death—was under God's control. Nothing could touch Him until the Father okayed it. No one could harm Him without God's permission.

That's true of God's children, too. When trouble comes our way, God hasn't lost control. He's in that situation with us, guiding our steps and sharing our sorrow. Don't forget the many times you've slipped through the crowd, as God has smoothed the way and made life simpler. He's saved you from harm because He had another plan, and a cliff wasn't in it. He's in control, no matter what happens.

Lord, whatever happens to me,
I'm glad you're in control.

True Kindness

A gift is as a precious stone in the eyes of him that hath it: withersoever it turneth, it prospereth.
PROVERBS 17:8

The rain was coming down in sheets now, and she had no idea how to change a flat. As long as it was raining so hard she held out little hope of getting someone to stop and help her. Suddenly she heard a tap on her window.

"Need some help?"

"I've got a flat, and I don't know how to fix it."

"You go wait with my wife in my car, and I'll have it changed in a jiffy."

Her savior was a young man with a beard and a kind face. He worked quickly in the pouring rain, and when he was finished he was drenched to the bone. She thanked him and began to pull a twenty dollar bill out of her wallet, but he refused to take it.

"Do something nice for someone else, and we'll call it square," he said.

True kindness doesn't look for any rewards. It is done from the heart, and there is no payment great enough to cover it. It is only when we learn from it and then give it to someone else that kindness is repaid. Giving of ourselves to others is a precious gift, and when we give it, it just keeps on going.

Help me to give kindness, love, and care, Father. Bless my effort, that my gift may grow and spread. Amen.

Abundant Life

"The thief comes only to steal and kill and destroy; I have come that they may have life, and have it to the full."
JOHN 10:10 NIV

Abundant life, full of good things on this earth, spiritual peace and joy, and full, satisfying relationships—that's what God intends His people to have. But listen to the world, and you'd never know it. Non-Christians often portray Christians as narrow-minded, sad, or hopelessly idealistic.

Your life in Jesus is probably nothing like that. When your faith is alive and active, you can feel clean, right with your Maker, and richer for being in a relationship with Him. He's been working in your life to bring spiritual abundance, deeper understanding of Him and the world around you, and joy that doesn't stop when trouble enters the door.

Nonbelievers can't know any of that. You can tell them that loving Jesus is the best thing ever, and they may think you're crazy. They've never experienced anything like it, so they can't imagine such peace and joy.

But one day the thief who came to steal, kill, and destroy their lives may make them so miserable that God's message can enter a crack in their armor against Him. They start to listen to His message of abundant life. Before long faith blossoms, and new life—abundant life—takes hold.

It's time to rejoice in Jesus.

Reasons to Give Thanks

THE LOVE OF FAMILY
And I will bless them that bless thee, and curse
him that curseth thee: and in thee shall all
families of the earth be blessed.
GENESIS 12:3

TRUE FRIENDS WHO ARE THERE
REGARDLESS OF CIRCUMSTANCES
A friend loveth at all times.
PROVERBS 17:17

GOD'S WORD, THE BREAD OF LIFE
It is written, that man shall not live by bread alone,
but by every word of God.
LUKE 4:4

God's Friend

"But you, O Israel, my servant, Jacob, whom I have chosen, you descendants of Abraham my friend, I took you from the ends of the earth, from its farthest corners I called you. I said, 'You are my servant'; I have chosen you and have not rejected you."
ISAIAH 41:8–9 NIV

Have you pondered the idea that, like Israel, the Lord of the universe is your friend? Perhaps you've been stopped in your tracks by the awe of that truth. *Why should He care for me?* you may wonder.

God chooses His friends on His own terms. The famous, the extraordinarily intelligent, the powerful aren't always on His list. Yet some of the most unexpected folks are. He doesn't choose based on worldly greatness. His own sense of mercy defines the choice, in ways we cannot now understand.

Many blessings follow friendship with God, but so do challenges. The Creator expects much of His friends, just as He gives much. Being a friend of Jesus requires that we suffer, struggle, and face numerous challenges, physical and spiritual. It's not the kind of thing He offers lightly or that we should accept blindly.

But when God chooses a friend, it's for forever. He never gives up or changes His mind. He's with you for this lifetime and eternity. Along with all the purely delightful things in His hand, He offers strength in trials and guidance for a long, hard way.

That's the best friendship anyone could offer.

Brimming with His Spirit

May God give you more and more mercy,
peace, and love.
JUDE 2 NLT

What a blessing, to continually receive more and more of God's mercy, peace, and love. That's just the kind of Christian life we'd like to have—until we're bursting with these good spiritual experiences, to the point where we simply can't hold them in.

Maybe we have already received so much from God. Our lives have changed drastically because of the salvation He offered. But bursting? Perhaps we wouldn't use *that* word to describe ourselves.

That's because God doesn't overfill us with His blessings. He gives us enough to share, then waits to see what we do with it. God gives blessings so we can encourage, teach, and lead others into a relationship with Him. He doesn't give them so that we can bulge with His unused gifts.

But if we receive God's gifts and pass them on to others, take hold of His Word and teachings, and use them to show others how to live, God fills us again.

When we've made that our lifestyle, we are truly blessed—and so are others who come in contact with us. Their growth in turn touches others' lives—and on and on it goes. The joys of mercy, peace, and love abound, just as God planned.

God Provides

Honour the LORD with thy substance, and with the firstfruits of all thine increase: So shall thy barns be filled with plenty, and thy presses shall burst out with new wine.
PROVERBS 3:9–10

A poor woman approached two men asking for money to buy bread for her children. The first man scowled and said, "I work hard for my money. Go and do the same for yourself and for your family!" The woman began to walk away, but the other man stopped her and said, "Poor woman, take this money, for it is not really mine. I do work hard for it, but it is by God's grace that I have it at all. If I give to you, I simply give to God what He has provided."

It is good to remember that without God we would not possess the things we do. All things come to us from God, and it is good that we share them. Jesus tells us that whenever we come to the aid of another person in need, we are in fact aiding Him. True prosperity comes only when we learn to give to others as freely as God gives to us.

Oh Father, soften my heart to those who are less fortunate than I am. Help me to appreciate the blessings I have been given and to share from my abundance. Amen.

Real Wisdom

Counsel is mine, and sound wisdom:
I am understanding; I have strength.
PROVERBS 8:14

Solomon was considered to be the wisest of all human beings. His judgment was sound and fair. Subjects traveled from all over Israel to seek his counsel. His word was law because people believed there was no greater mind in all the world. Solomon did nothing more than use the gifts God had given him in the best way possible. He prayed long and hard for God to inspire him with special wisdom.

Solomon was able to give great wisdom because he was in touch with the source of wisdom: God. As much as Solomon was willing to give himself to God, God was willing to give Himself right back. God showed that He was willing to do the same for us by giving Himself in the person of His Son, Jesus Christ. All we need to do is accept His gift and try to the best of our ability to follow His example. Like Solomon, we receive strength and understanding from the God who gives us all good things.

Lord, I wish I could be one with Your Spirit, that I might spread Your will in this world. You offer so much, and I take so little. Help me to use what You hold forth, that I might reflect the blessed light of Your Son, Jesus Christ, throughout this world. Amen.

Thank You, God, for Everything

Thank You, God, for everything—
the big things and the small—
For every good gift comes from God,
the giver of them all.
And so at this time we offer up a prayer
To thank You, God, for giving us
a lot more than our share.
First, thank You for the little things
that often come our way—
The things we take for granted
and don't mention when we pray—
The unexpected courtesy, the thoughtful, kindly deed,
A hand reached out to help us
in the time of sudden need.
Then thank You for the miracles
we are much too blind to see,
and give us new awareness
of our many gifts from Thee.
And help us to remember that the key to life and living
Is to make each prayer a prayer of thanks
and each day a day of thanksgiving.

HELEN STEINER RICE

Who to Thank

Give thanks unto the LORD, call upon his name, make known his deeds among the people. Sing unto him, sing psalms unto him, talk ye of all his wondrous works.
1 CHRONICLES 16:8–9

Is Thanksgiving a joyful time for you? It can be, if you're focused on the One who deserves your thanks. But often we become so wrapped up in a large turkey dinner, a family get-together, and other holiday celebrations that we lose our joy.

Though the Pilgrims have been stereotyped as sour-faced folks, that image is wrong. When they had a successful harvest in 1621, they just had to rejoice. Some men went out to shoot game for their harvest celebration table, and the Pilgrims invited the Wampanoag Indians. Their celebration lasted three days. Though no formal religious service was part of the first celebration, Edward Winslow, who wrote a letter to England about it, reported that it was by God's goodness that the small band of Christians was far from want. They knew who to thank.

So make Thanksgiving a time of joy when you remember the blessings of God. Whether you're joining a large family or celebrating alone, it's a time to remember the love that's brought you to this point in your life.

Say one big "thanks" to God.

Thank You, Lord, for the blessing of Your love.
Keep me faithful in thanks all year long.